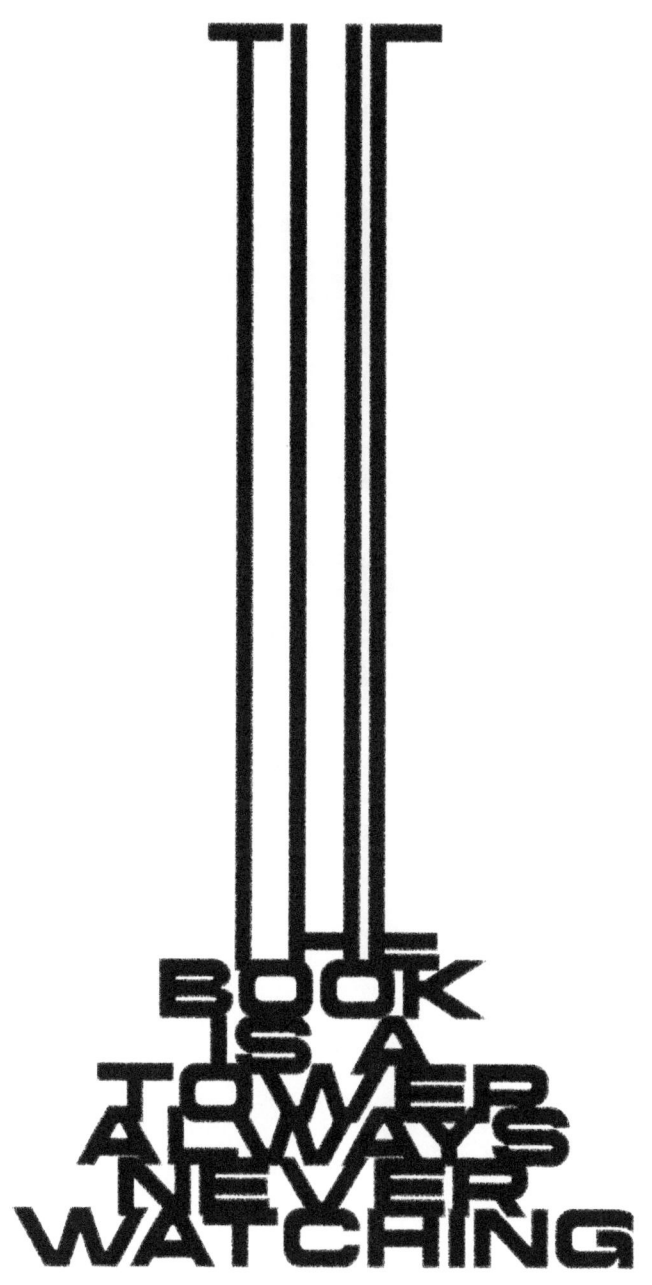

Copyright © Rachel Zavecz 2024
The Book is a Tower Always Never Watching

Published by CLOAK.wtf
ISBN: 979-8-218-52758-7

RACHEL ZAVECZ

THE BOOK IS A TOWER ALWAYS WATCHING

IS

NEVER

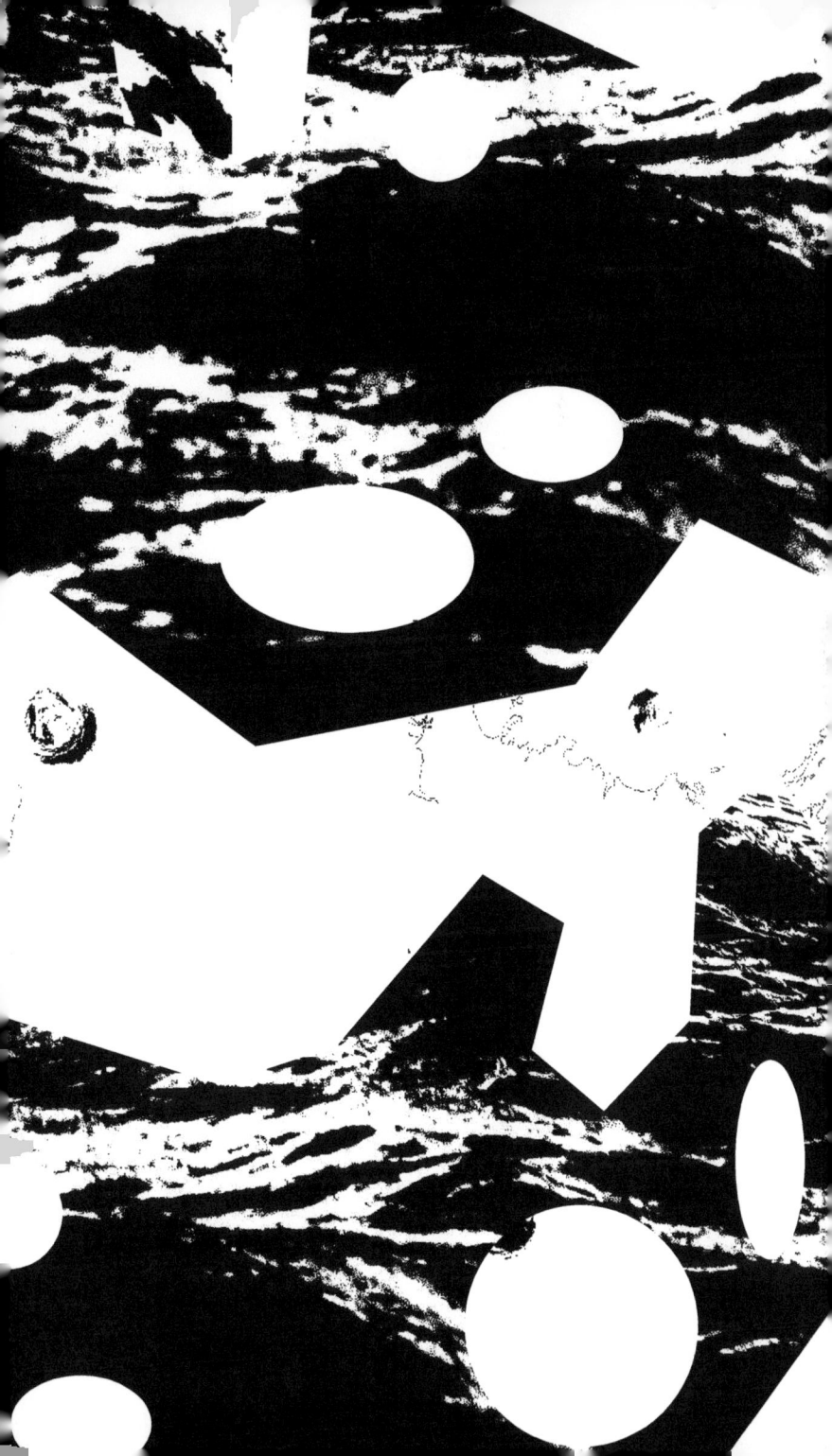

INTRODUCTION

A BRIEF COMPILATION OF DOCUMENTS TRANSCRIBED
722.23.6790021 AG - 700.24.6790021 AG

TIMEFRAME: APPROACHING CYCLE REBOOT
BETWEEN MACHINE #23 AND MACHINE #24

AUTOMATIZATION

the farthest continent there is a gentle sliding of tectonics which lends itself to alc

tories [: *production* *and* *progress*], d

spliced *angels* *kissing* *body* *parts* *with* *their* *scalpel-*

gers] note. "there must always be one that acl

cess" a smoky skin sheath swallowing light auto

stly mechanized base organic parts segn

silver-jointed *skeletons* *and* *translucent* *wiring*].

atomybecomesthenewautomatonassemblingfleshandmetalsintothemostefficienthumantran

next *comes* *the* *new* *perfection*

of   precision

   [:
skeleton   and

                    assembling meat

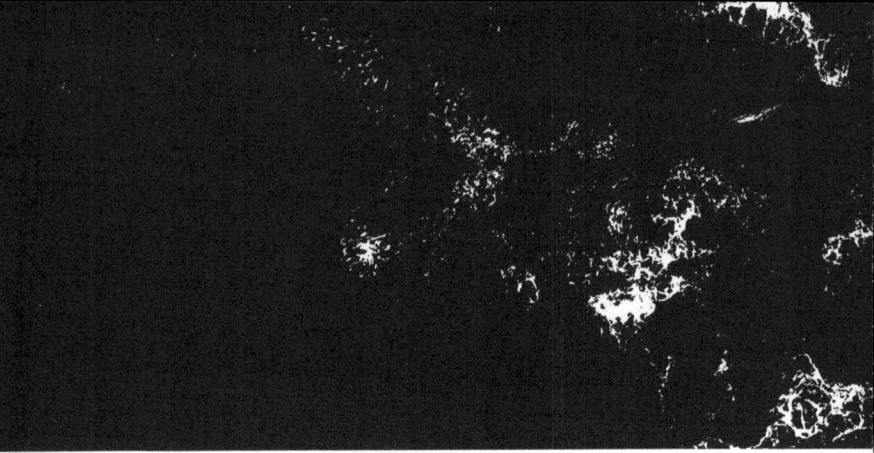

[suspending bones like museum mobile, builds
striated segments of the newest body: the
child-physician threads each slender segment
with silver wire to frame a greater machine]

heavy smell like a velvet curtain
hangs between each downy molten feather
black strings of dewy chain.
link.
form.
blood.pearls dripping softly into
one.
zillion pale.lashed cat.eyes

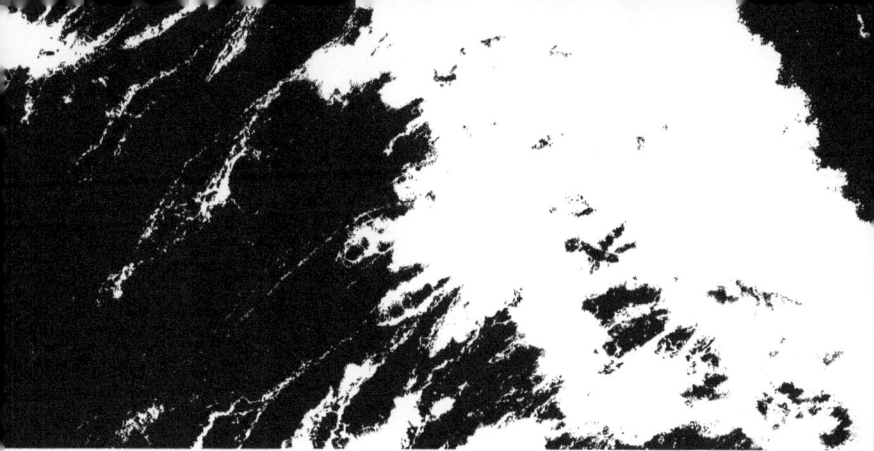

[carefully extracting eyes with surgical scalpel,
sews each into the burnished wing: the child-
physician prepares for future production]

one result is every tiny golden eye pierced through
by a slender silver pushpin

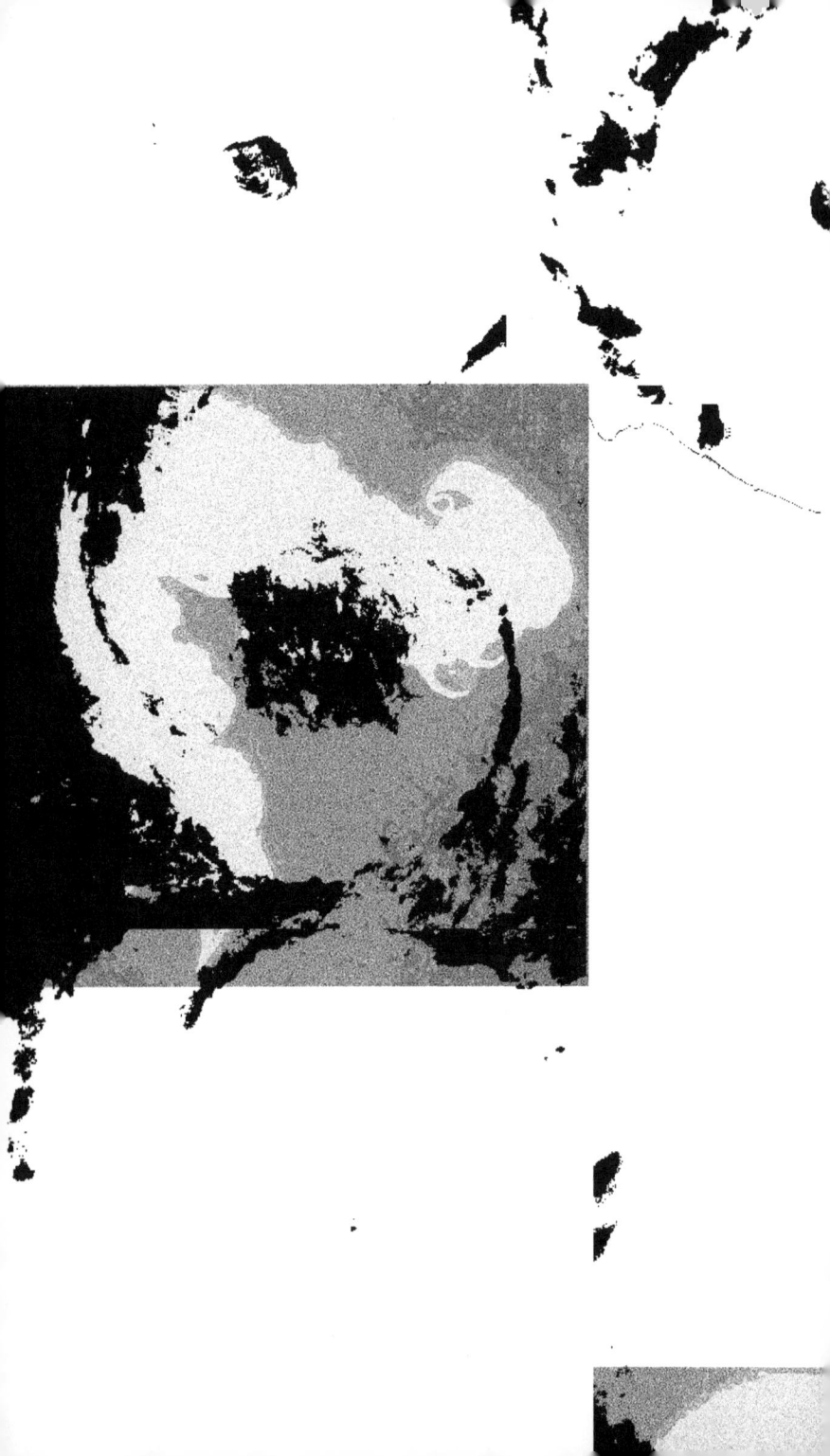

dark

black-sheathed and translucent silver boned

red-maned

primarily metallic

the lattice.work. of his veins
at.
the
jointed
click
of his hund/red hands
(500 fingers!)
is.
a
mult.iplic.ation of num.bers.
too
comp.lex
to
cal.cu.late

he

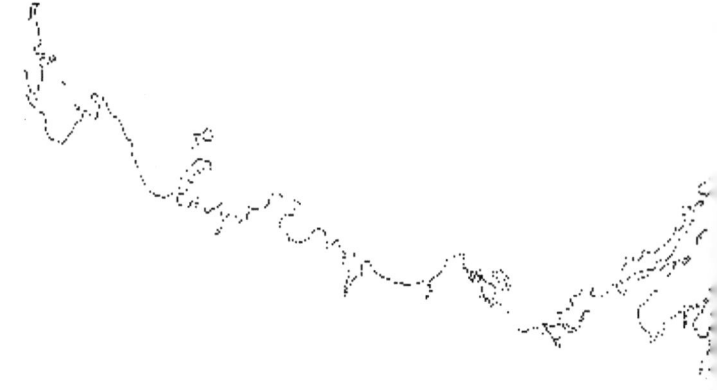

is.

in(to)/with
pix.els
and mega.byte.s
and
the rational-random
generat.ion
of the compute(r)/
mach.in.e
is.hands.
and
cyber.net.ic
tongue(ing)

e is the spider today, darkly golden carapace, jointed forelimbs, no chrys apery or transscaled membrane-

ere is only the sucking stomach

d seeping under the glittering exoskeletal

her outer

says, "you are a megamachine you area goddess"

is satisfied for no one challenges her righteou

has built the perfect

frame of unparalleled refinement

compound

such facet and refraction that as she crawls inside o

er face flickers molten into a thousand needles of synthetic love darkly

of

refraction

into   needles

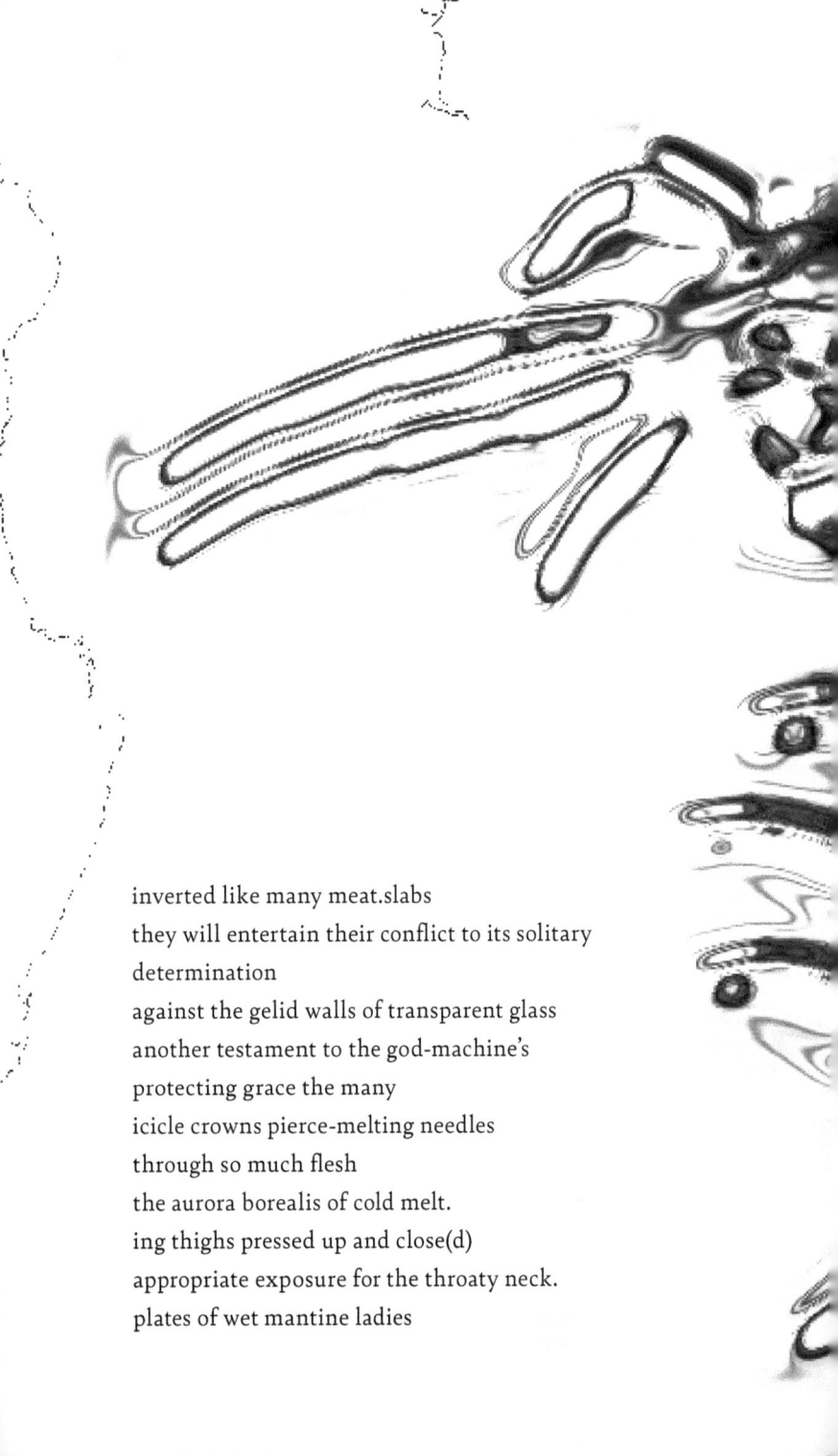

inverted like many meat.slabs
they will entertain their conflict to its solitary
determination
against the gelid walls of transparent glass
another testament to the god-machine's
protecting grace the many
icicle crowns pierce-melting needles
through so much flesh
the aurora borealis of cold melt.
ing thighs pressed up and close(d)
appropriate exposure for the throaty neck.
plates of wet mantine ladies

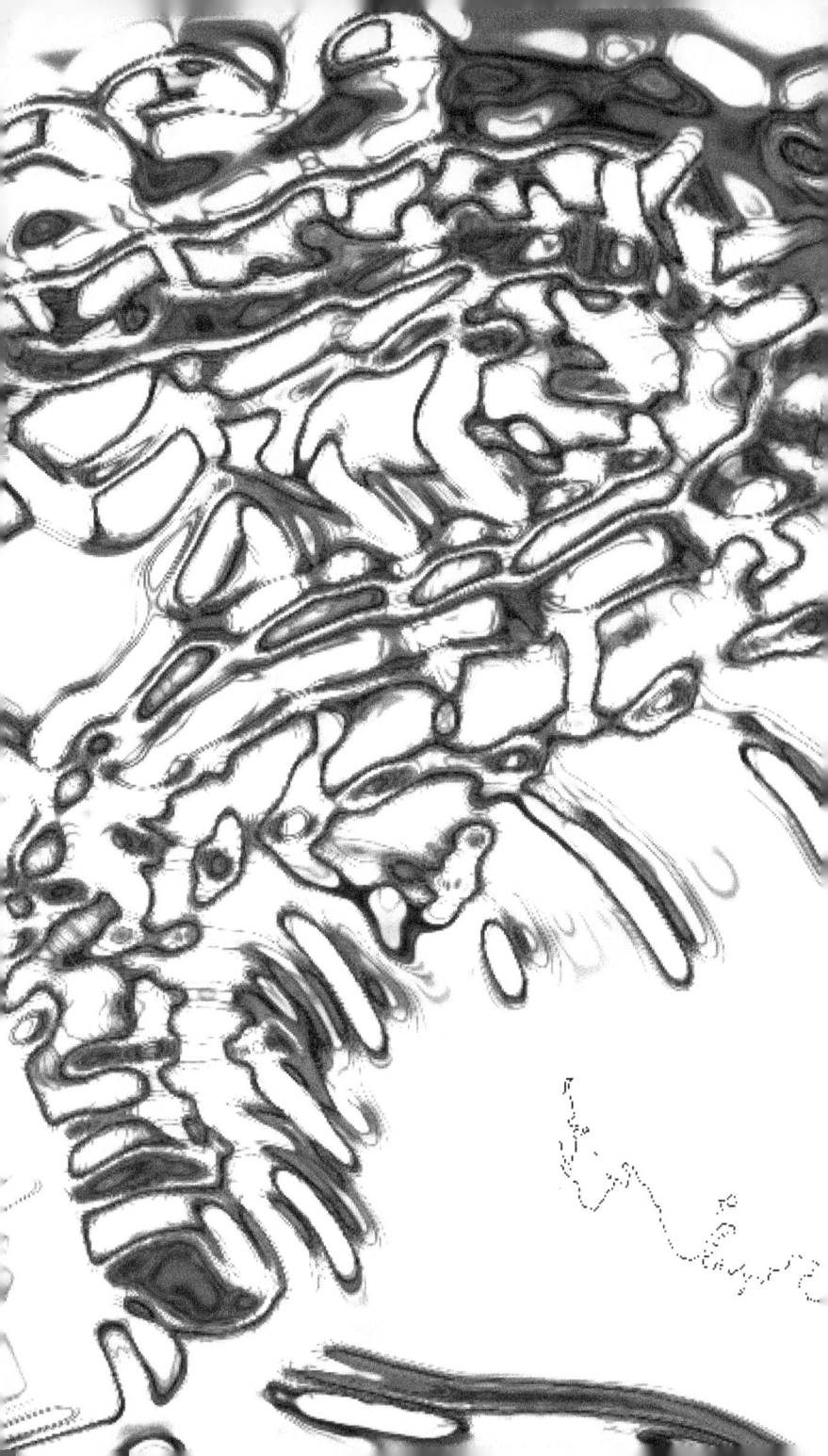

centi.pede s.mack
ing
wide
and salivating out the.

click.

gold.en stomachs   sweat.
+lilac overlapping. rims
th?e

click.

              5hund.red
    lidded
eye?. want.   =

click.

1thousand.   bodies-
sliding slow a.cross a
              flick.er.ing
      sc.ree?n   he

click.

match.es mewling. limb to
        her. cyber-
flesh
        +tear.ing
m?ath.e
m.atic?ally.
        with poison

click.

        chrom.a.tic   scales
inter.lock?ing
& unknowing
        here.

click.

is.   the   per.fect.ion
in
pixel?s

she [...] finger between the plates of her diamond-cut car [...]

[...] against the cool plateglass and the coldness of the outer

[...] the movement of two interlocked machines [...] say

[...] must operate carefully - there are scriptures to be follo[...]

[...] the many hands glisten with her varnish the piercing organs of his mouth are m[...]

[...] sun-capped teeth incisors magnetized by her gigabytes an algorithm which has re[...]

[...]timate levels of physiologic accuracy she is his closest match at 99.98787893 p[...]

between

                      the   coldness

                interlocked

hands

                                  99.98787893

a softset color palette

orange-skinned and black veined

she is glowing softly phantom

chrysanthemums already crowning

the sunset coils of her silky hair

IT IS THE WILL OF THE GOD-MACHINE THAT ALL
SPECTATORS REMAIN EQUIDISTANT FROM THE DOME ON ALL
SIDES BY SEVERAL SEGMENTS OF STANDARD MEASUREMENT

such comforting authority to the hundred thousand people
pressing white fingers to their pale-lashed faces
wide camera lens.eyes trembling saying,
"oh, how sad the will the god-machine must fall
so hard
upon these
tender.izing peoples" a dark fusion of
kitten
eyes
and chicken.wire
rubs dry
scrapes
along the corneas
of a physician's
tender

e nearly drove his tooth into her eye" says gold fluttering nervously against the m

ish of the glass it is always nervous in these situations there is a dialogue which fol

SILVER: stay calm it is such a modern thing JEWEL-STUDDED:

are most modern to be sure SILVER: such an intimate gathering

reveal what lies within the shell JEWEL-STUDDED: there wil

developments SILVER: we all recall GOLD: there is a danger

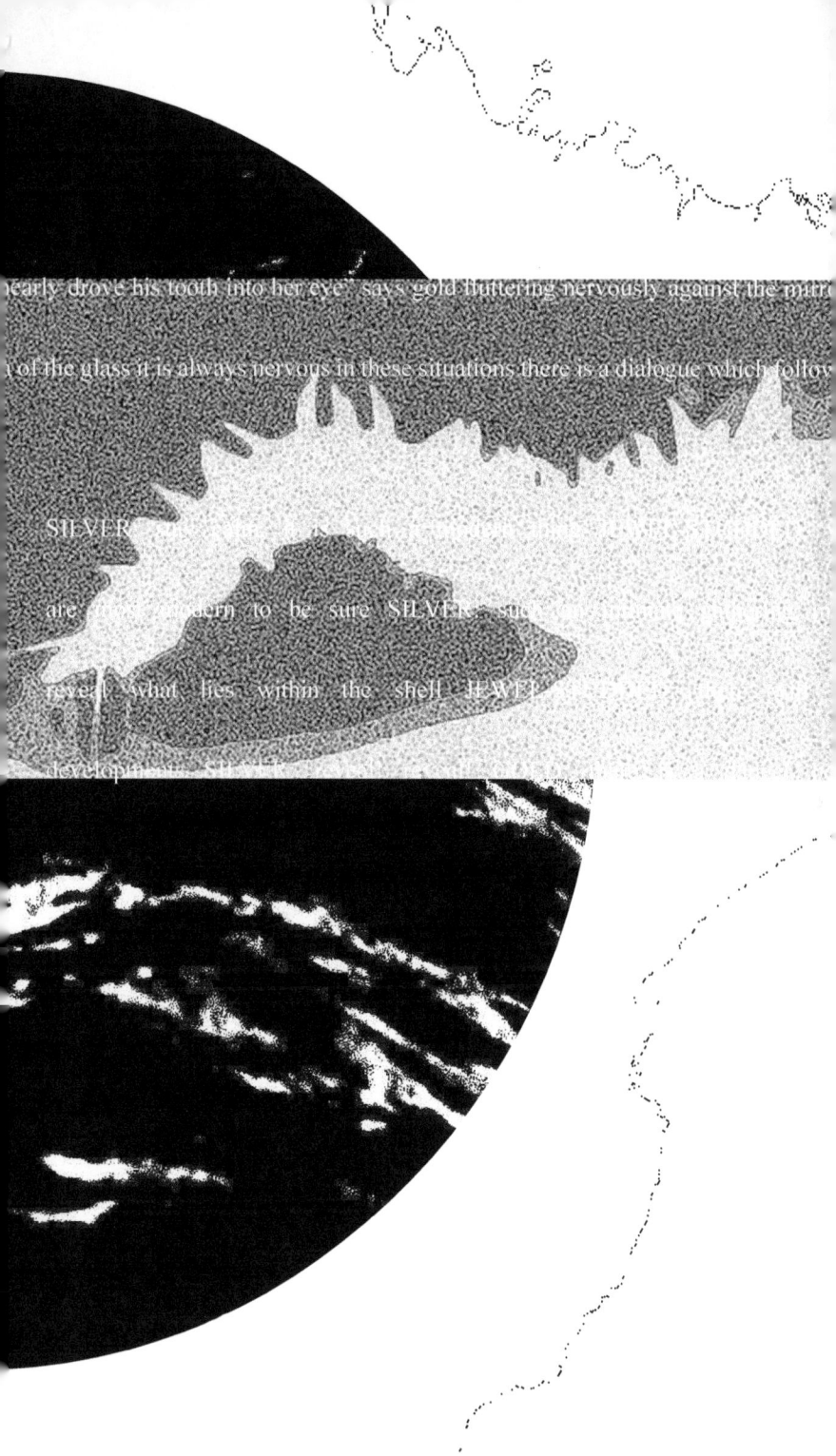

he says "you will be transformed! you will become the new and improved messiah! with 30,000 ziggawatts of power threaded through my megamachine you will become the superior god!"

"there are proteins" says the scientist with golden scissor-fingers, "there is science which suggests that manipulating these proteins will affect you on the extrasensory level!"

he is breathing hard, his glands are salivating,
the many golden eyes on his feathered wings are
blinking discordantly which he ignores

                                                              he is fervid

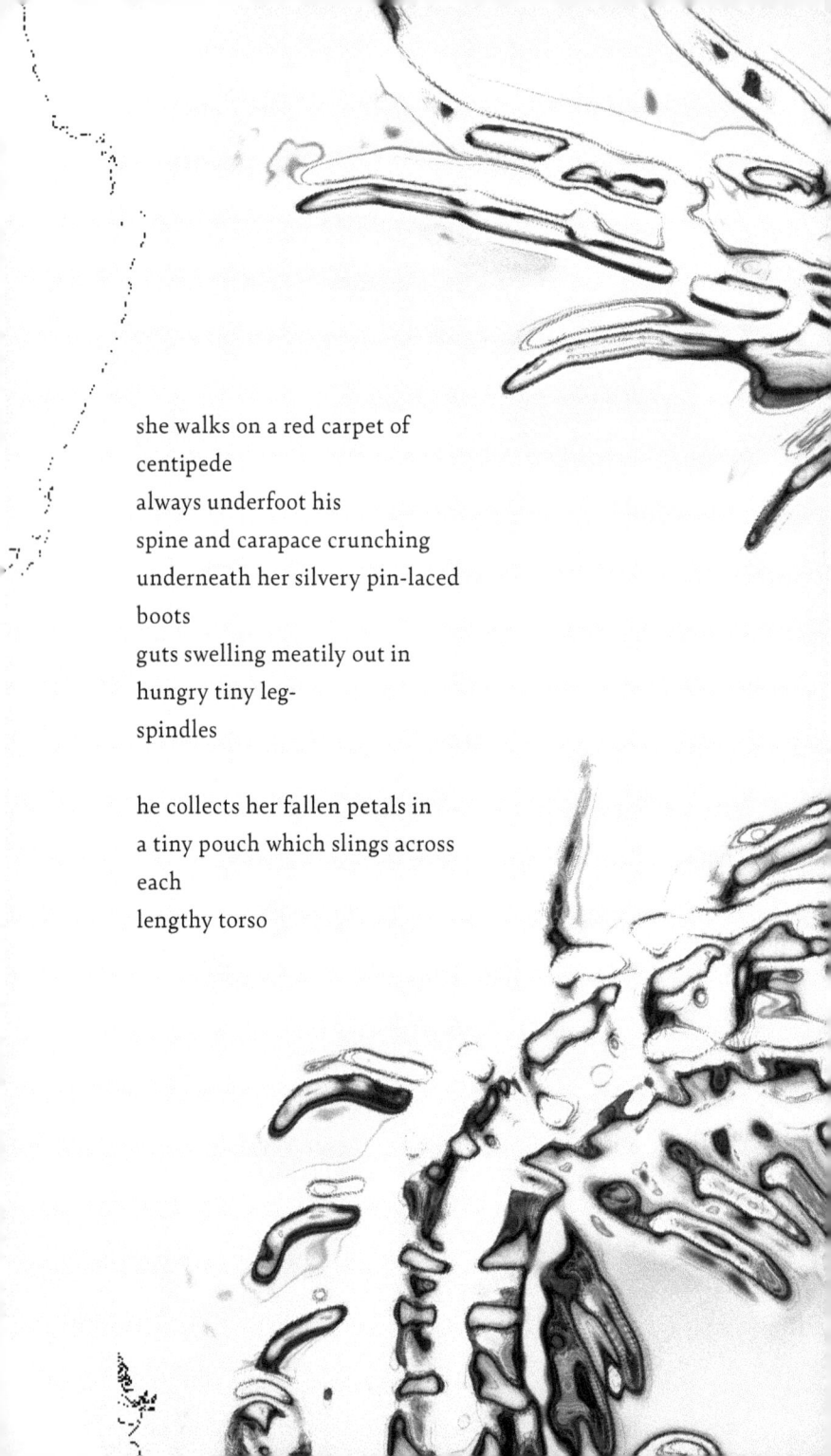

she walks on a red carpet of
centipede
always underfoot his
spine and carapace crunching
underneath her silvery pin-laced
boots
guts swelling meatily out in
hungry tiny leg-
spindles

he collects her fallen petals in
a tiny pouch which slings across
each
lengthy torso

mazon's hair, silver-crusted and violent red with filigree threaded through the entry

ands, the monstrous shapes which lend themselves to knotting around his jointed fi

brindled spines which must be smoothed from one direction

ir increasing luminous flux a challenge to the darkening

compound eye her glitter her refine

        interlude

                                        threaded through

                            smoothed

increasing

he is prostrate, gummy limbs wiggling uncontrollably
he says, "you will reform the universe into its most sublimate
design!"

the shadowy automaton has necrosed, it has become
silver-throated now it is
the baleful god-machine riddled
with tubules, cuts
a magnificent figure
reams celestial
atop the
darkly
shining
tower

oh   ekin"   says

e many hands so many hands of hiding in the most sentimental of ways, though
ed of poison for the [illegible] [illegible] says, "your luminosity will [illegible] a sec
rough your skeleton which [illegible] ds to your bronzed allure. [illegible] ungry soul
rabbling against the glass and [illegible] natch there [illegible] of utmost consisten

—

d   her   response   EJECT!   [illegible]   [illegible]   mouth   rec
ponse   ERROR   ERR   [illegible] D FUN

[illegible] says [illegible] he [illegible] says "uhhh" and feels ton

EJECT!   EJECT!

ERROR!   ERROR!   INVALID_FUNCTION

1000 needles crown
His face
of glassy teeth
magnesium and
phosphate
argon, sulfur, more
wending through
His titanic
silver laurels crown of
bristling metal(lic)
pain
there is always
black blood
for the god-machine
broze-ribbed and blazing
bright eyes
He will let go
of her only
when she crumbles
in-
to dust

(the chorus is silent)

after, He looks in(side)
her final moment — there is
copper-rusted eyes and
power,
needled crucifixion,
a crowning sun
Chrysanthemums are
wending beaten dusk in(to)
a circlet for
her nocturnal peak

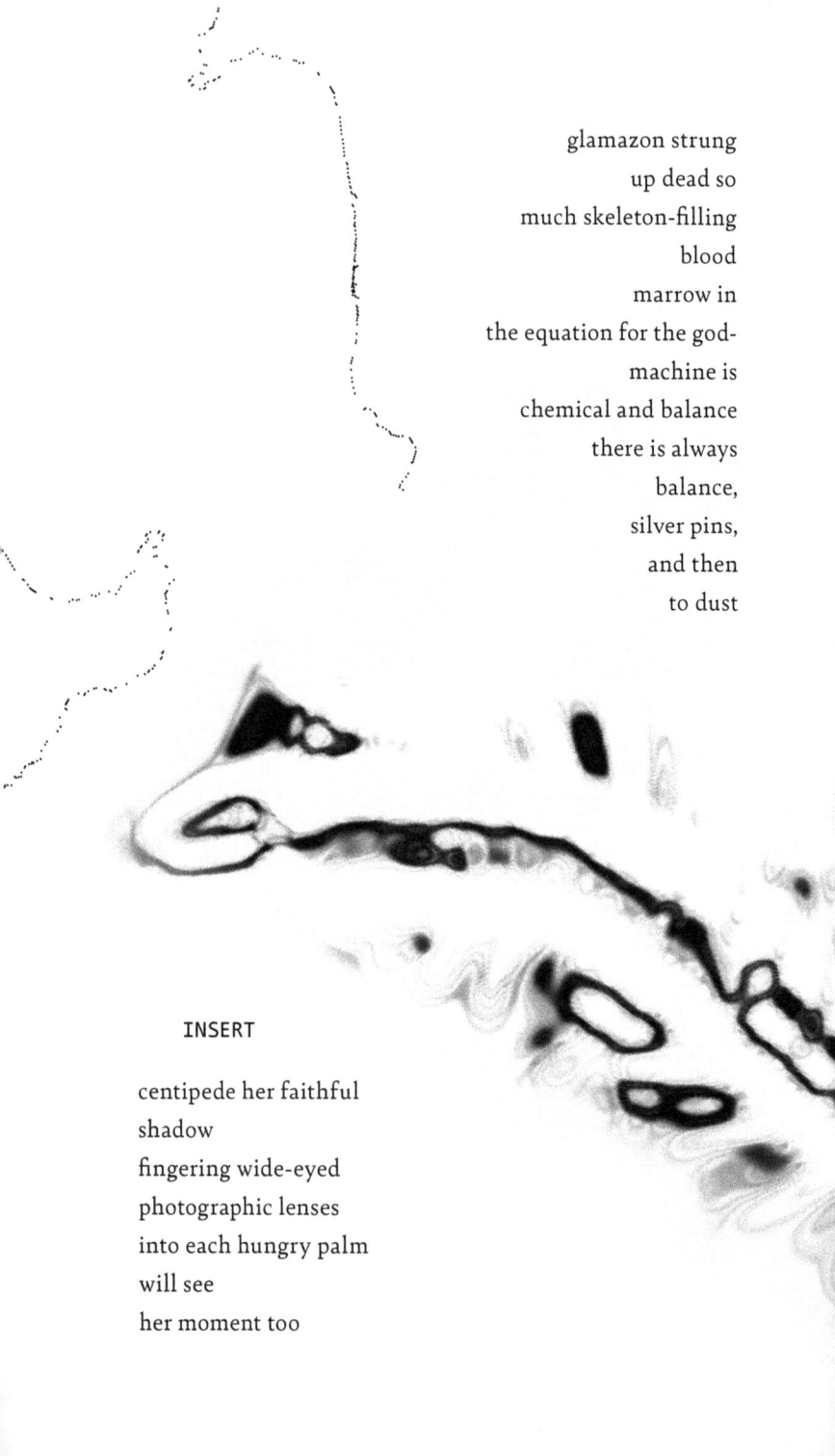

glamazon strung
up dead so
much skeleton-filling
blood
marrow in
the equation for the god-
machine is
chemical and balance
there is always
balance,
silver pins,
and then
to dust

INSERT

centipede her faithful
shadow
fingering wide-eyed
photographic lenses
into each hungry palm
will see
her moment too

when it is
over
he will gather
every slender limb

CYCLE REBOOT

He is procedure
He is solution
and He is only slightly weeping
clicks.
   cryst.all.ine jaws
        and.
    turns

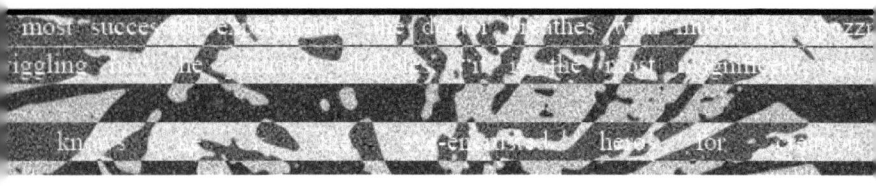

                              much less
               he primarily

he is the   creation of

END OF BODY

APPENDIX MATRIX

APPENDIX A

en.cap.sul.ate.d in
ice
slow-moving heart.
beat.
of stag.nat.ion pieces
there.
is stirring
beneath the sheets
sharp-edged and
scientific - aha!
the spiny veneer
of the dappled iron
hide
speaks soft the monster
please(d)! it takes
some guts
prodigious rolls
them around its tongue
so wet and yum
tells,
the difference between
death
and suspension
must. be.
a fashion
con.scious religion

APPENDIX B

MOTHS.
TODAY THE BLACK WITCH
TODAY THE PROMETHEA
TODAY THE LUNA
TODAY THE DYSDAEMONIA
TODAY THE SPANISH MOON
TODAY THE WHITE-LINED SPHINX
BUTTERFLIES.
TODAY THE ALPINE BLACK
TODAY THE EASTERN TIGER

OR.
TODAY ASCALAPHA ODORATA
TODAY CALLOSAMIA PROMETHEA
TODAY DYSDAEMONIA FOSTERI
TODAY ACTIAS LUNA
TODAY GRAELLSIA ISABELLAE
TODAY HYLES LINEATA

TODAY PAPILIO MAACKII
TODAY PAPILIO GLAUCUS

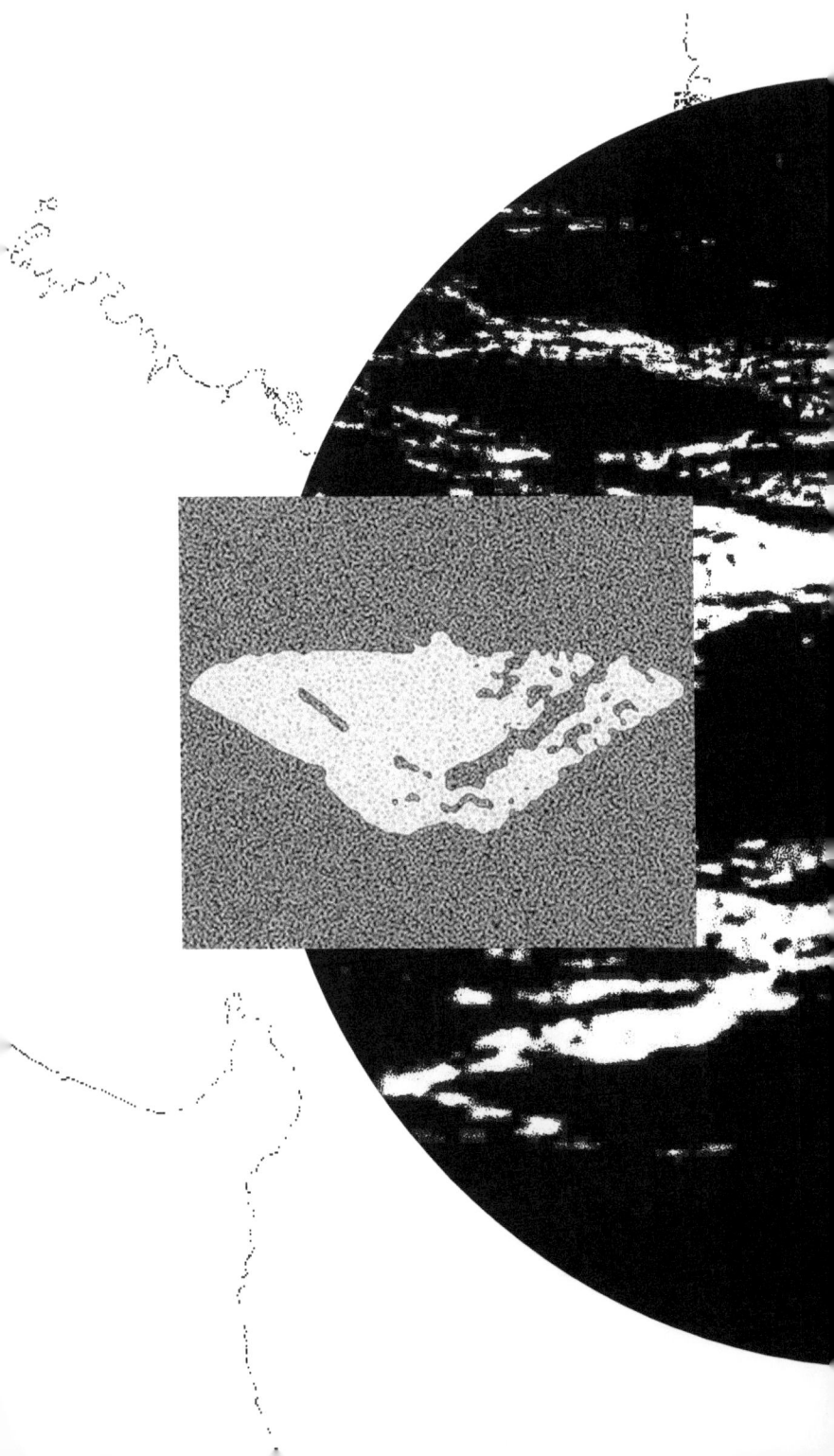

APPENDIX C

Outside of the Central Office of the Universal Scientific Anatomical Remodeling and Research Administration (USARRA).

753.23.6790021 AG, universal schism timeframe.

A Monument.

tall cylindrical spires of recycled crystalline chemistry
needle up at the center of the universe
they are hard-edged dripping vitriol, they are the
quintessence of quintessence
they are polite
they are the broken glass eyeteeth which protrude from the
skeletal remains of the once almighty god-machine
the behemoth corpse still rusting silver blood

"I've had a fantastic idea," the god-machine had said, only
moments pre-demise. "I will slow the expansion of the
universe, and bring everything to light"
and the people had erupted into great clamity:

> THE PEOPLE: with light?!
> THE GOD: with light
> THE PEOPLE: but light?!
> THE GOD: be still!
> THE PEOPLE: we are not made for light
> THE GOD: nocturnal sensibilities will fade
> THE PEOPLE: see how He intrudes on our sensibilities!

"Incorrigible god - He is contaminated!" they exclaimed, spitting out the silver blood, "He has gone mad and must be stopped!"

and as the colossal frame of the god-machine reared, dark outer-shell plates sliding mellifluous past one another and the burnished amaranthine finish of His carapace glowed ominously dark,
the people muttered angrily

"we constructed you" they said, "we can topple you and raise another in your place, a much more malleable god"

the god-machine spouted static and His insides screeched:

```
UNHANDLED EXCEPTION HAS OCCURRED IN YOUR
APPLICATION. IF YOU CHOOSE CONTINUE, THE
APPLICATION WILL IGNORE THIS ERROR AND ATTEMPT TO
CONTINUE. IF YOU CHOOSE DELETE, THE APPLICATION
WILL CLOSE IMMEDIATELY.
```

"DELETE! DELETE!"

then, "I am dead" the god-machine had stated wearily, "but the expansion of the universe will be slowed before I crystallize"

"not so - for He is dead!" they had cried as the god-machine fell, hard edges shivering

and they fell into the crevasse He created as He crashed, dying and shrieking most embarrassingly

the geometric prowess of the spires is not lost on the automaton
gaping lustily at the hexagonal plaque which relates this
historical significance
he is unabashed with static wonder
at the glow of artificial heart-light and tasteful crystal shrubbery
which forms a delicate ring around the needle-teeth

"centrally they exist in twelve dimensions
five of which are crushing blackness
molten star-guts and gaseous vapor" say the pale-faced people
they are enlightened people
they are scientific

"what exists?"
"the spires" they say
and their heads are shaking at the automaton because
they have seen his kind before
he is a half-life, every fraction of his existence halved
then halved
then halved
then halved
and on

how charming he is, they think
he will make an ingenious test subject
for the well-reputed doctor

ACKNOWLEDGMENTS

This book would not have been possible without the early encouragement of Lara Glenum, the guidance and expertise of Amy Thompson, and the visionary design work of Mike Corrao.

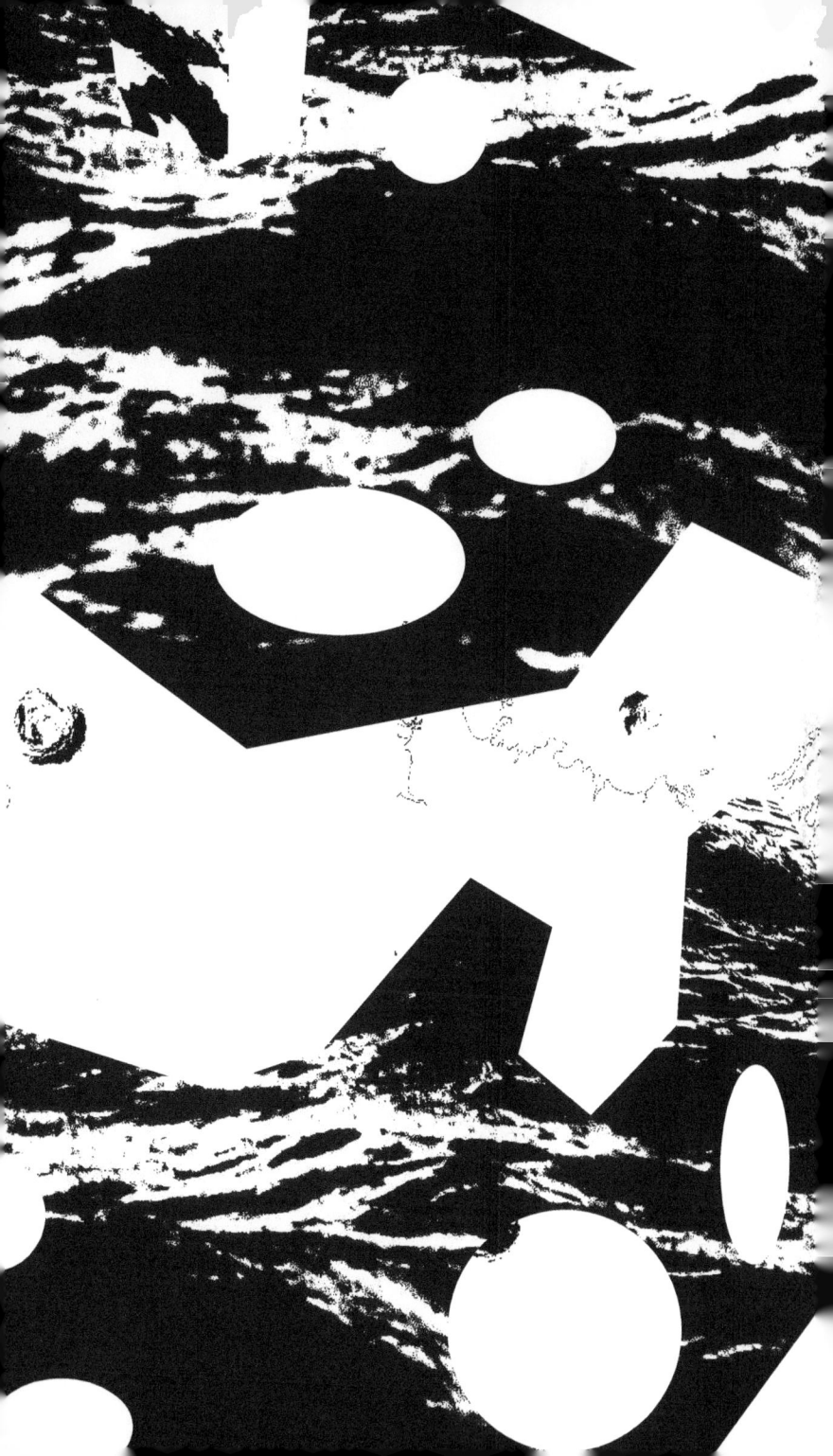

CLOAK

Learn more at http://cloak.wtf

www.ingramcontent.com/pod-product-compliance
Lightning Source LLC
LaVergne TN
LVHW052049070526
838201LV00086B/5188